To My Bro.

I

WAS

VOICELESS

Thanx for your
Support & Love
Trina 5/30/30

By

Katrina Powell

Acknowledgements

I want to let my son Kyril know that I appreciate him for editing my book, and for all of the time and energy he has put into my dream. I want to say, thank you to my cousin Rasshida for lending her eyes, time and talent to my art work. I want to thank my mother for opening my eyes to my gift, I miss you so much. To my kingdom sisters for holding me accountable, especially Eiram Roby and Dara Motivates. I thank my heavenly father for sitting with me and birthing the woman in front of you today.

Introduction

I wrote this book to reflect my forty-one years of love, pain, laughter, of every emotion I have ever felt, carried around and couldn't let go of until I was no longer voiceless. Voiceless because I doubted how Dope I was. I let life's obstacles and self-doubt hinder me from sharing my gift. I know I'm not the only woman who has talked down to herself. I want to share my voice and say, **"WE CAN DO IT"**. Step into your blessing.

I Was Voiceless, is a poetry book about life experiences, told in the only way I could speak. As you read these collections of poems, I hope that they inspire you, make you laugh, and help you to take a chance on your dreams.

Dedication

I want to thank God for giving me the ability to express myself with words. Thank you to my son's Ka'Quan and Kyril for being my strength and for always believing in me. We are the 3K's and I will forever be grateful that God allowed me to be your mother. Thanks Ebony for all of your encouraging words and for staying on me to share my voice with the world. This book is also dedicated to the many talented women who feel voiceless and scared to make a move ....I say walk in your faith not by sight. Let God's plans for you be brighter than your fears!

Table of Contents

Chapter One
PRAYERS

Chapter Two
KIN

Chapter Three
SURVIVAL

Chapter Four
MOTIVATION

Chapter Five

SELF

Chapter Six

DEDICATIONS

Chapter Seven
REFLECTION

Chapter Eight
FREE STYLE

Chapter One

PRAYERS

God

He has BESTOWED his love amongst us

His LOYALTY is ultimate

His company is always EMBRACED

His STORY is our platform

Our SPIRITS dwell in his sanctuary

His IMPRESSIONS are left beside us

He is a NECESSITY in our lives

He is GENUINE

In the beginning

In the middle

In the end

He is a BLESSING!

His House

In the house of the lord,

Many come to give their praise to him

Many come to hear his words,

Of all the reasons they come

To love the lord

To make him their first love

To say, thank you

Without God the necessities of life are meaningless

With God you always have a father and a friend

You may not see him visually,but you may

Feel him emotionally

With God you know when the sun beams

His house is extremely happy

With God you know when the rain falls

He is weeping for us

When it storms

He is fighting to save us

I sit in the Lord's house

I am grateful and my love for him

Is unconditional.

Katrina Powell

Father

I come displeased with myself

I make excuses for ill actions

I say, "thank you", with resentment

I say, "I love you", with a hint of hatred

Father,

I pray for only self

I chant my anger to those who listen

I believe that I'm broken

Empty space amongst collectors

Father,

For all my misguided fury; it is controlled by something greater

For all the pain that has been placed in my way

I travel with it for strength

Father,

You taught me patience when I knew none

You taught me to hear in a loud world

You taught me to search below the skin, to find enchanted beauty

You taught me to laugh when tears fall like landslides

I was voiceless

Father,

You taught me that with faith

You walk with many

You are never alone.

Katrina Powell

A Note To

My God-

I hear you talking to me

Weighing heavy on my heart

Tears sliding from my eyes

Unaware that my soul isn't well

I continue on;

Ignoring the echo in my ear

Being stubborn to my wants

Realizing I have betrayed you-

Still you wrap me, console me

Like any father,

Whose daughter has disobeyed

I won't say, "I don't know"

Honestly, I just feel it's my moment

Then I feel like I'm beyond my moment

I withdraw-

I let the devil distract me

I let him torch my hopes

I was voiceless

I come back on bending knees

Tearful eyes

Asking for you to forgive

A sinner.

Katrina Powell

Fighting with the Devil

Every morning is a blessing

Although on Sunday, I get this tingle

This feeling overwhelms me

I toss, I can't sleep

I go back and forth

Then I walk into his house

All the torment slips away

Like a baby falling asleep

Then I reflect on the days before

And I try to repent on what I have done

And what I have said-

I can't change time

So, I claim my wrongs

I say to God I will try harder

I will be that light you talk about

Fighting with the devil is a full time job

Loving you is unconditional

Even though I leave home

I was voiceless

Shielded and knowing

I let him pick at my weaknesses

And I bend

Sunday I come to testify

That I am a sinner

Fighting the devil

Is the battle I'm trying to win.

Katrina Powell

Chatting

God

You have given me choices

You have given me two great spirits

You have given me two of me to nurture

Though, you only gave me one heart to love with

One soul for a ran down body

You have walked me through the gutters

Only you can help me choose,

Only you can give me guidance when it is dark

You have spoken to me in the most amazing ways

You have even visited me

Could you please guide my heart?

Where my feet and head won't go

Could you tell me your thoughts?

For your opinion always matters.

I was voiceless

Happy Soul

My soul is happy

Every time I see white pillow clouds

Different shades of blue afloat

The vision of my boys beaming back

The voice of Damian in my ear

My soul is grateful

That I'm loved

That I have shelter

That someone prayed for me

My soul is satisfied

For what I have

For my health,

For my children

For my faith

My soul has made me whole

The body will prosper

The mind will regulate

My spiritual love is strong

I have no doubt in God

Katrina Powell

I have no doubt,

He can turn my tears into smiles

I have no doubt,

He can take my pain and dissolve it

I have no doubt in his abilities

My soul is happy.

Dear Father

Peace

I come bowed and with a broken heart,

For the many murdered lives,

For the many families and friends who are grieving

God, I ask you to open your arms wide to shelter

Our lost and fallen children

To remove the pain and fill that space with peace

Peace to rise after the chaos

Peace to forgive those, unable to see they are worthy of your love

Peace to speak faith into those that time has harden

That have forgotten your devotion in the midnight hour

That have replaced being thankful for just another day

God, I am asking you to build up the weak

To revise the strong and let thy spirit

Be gathered in harmony,

For peace is bright but quiet

Peace is Innocent

Peace is the time when God reveals to us

How unique we are when we choose God.

Amen.

Chapter Two

KIN

In My Life

You may not give me everything I desire

You may not treat me the way I want at times

You are MOM

You are always gonna be a part of my life

No matter how many times I wish you away

No matter how many times I scream-

I hate you or leave me alone

You are going to be a part of my life

You are always in my corner

Picking up my broken pieces

Being my friend when I'm in trouble

Being my mom when I rebel

Being who you really are

My mom

There aren't too many moms like you

Taking on the battle like a champion

Fighting the war against opposition

I commend you for your courage

I commend you for your strength

I commend you for being you

My mom

Love you.

Sisters& Brothers

My sisters and brothers are the greatest part of my life

They make it where I love to see the next day

Proud to say, there are little ones under me

I care for them more than their dads

Its pure love and care that I have

I pray to God time after time

To keep them healthy and wise

When situations occur that they can't handle

I am here to help

Sometimes I think I would be dead

If it wasn't for my siblings

Creating these lives took some work

Thank you, Linette

For understanding I needed company along this journey

You don't have to be the best parent

As long as your love is pure

Guaranteed to stay within us

As you push us to the finish line

Being the oldest child

Also means being a parent and a friend at times

Being a guide

On the path of life experiences

Lending them a hand when needed

Showing them life is full of surprises

I want to be the one who

Teaches them obstacles may come

And when they do-

They'll always have their sisters and brothers

Through trials and tribulations

They are your points of strength.

Mothers

For centuries there have been mothers
A woman who has been foundation for families
A woman that will give herself
To obtain the goals for her children
For decades it has been a mother's oath
To instill a faith into her children
To love them unconditionally
To teach them the basics of the world
Education, manners, and most of all respect
To provide them with shelter,food and clothing
For as long as time has been
There has been a mother's hugs and kisses
With her promise never to leave, unless you ask
Knowing she is lurking in the shadows
Keeping her promise to show up, she is always a mother
She made a promise to always protect you
Even during the times when you are being difficult
There a mother will remain with outreached arms
For as long as time goes
There will be a woman
Her second nature will be a Mother.

Katrina Powell

A Mother's Child

A child of my own,
A child to cuddle when he cries
A child to hold in my arms
A child to call my own
A child that rises like the sun
A child that grows like planted seeds
A child that blossoms like sunflowers
A child of my own,
The child I will teach positive from negative
The child I will love unconditionally
The child I will worry about after he's grown
A child of my own
The child I've raised to be an individual
The child I have given birth to is my very own
The child I will teach that nothing is impossible
A child of my own,
The worries of being his parent
The concern of the life he leads
The depth of my love for him
Will show–
A child of my own.

Lifetouch

I GOT A DAY

TO WASH AND FEED YOU

I GOT A DAY

TO PREPARE YOU

TO SAY HELLO AND GOODBYE

I GOT A DAY

TO GIVE YOU MEMORIES OF A LIFETIME

I GOT A DAY

TO REMIND YOU WHY YOU SPECIAL

I GOT A DAY

TO EXPRESS MY FAITH IN YOU

I GOT A DAY

TO TELL YOU ANGRY IS LONELY

Katrina Powell

I GOT A DAY

WITH LIFE

SO, LET TODAY NOT BE IN VAIN.

Mommy's Little Boys

When I was going through nine months of motherhood

Nobody said, Daddy's little boys

It was mommy's little boys

I carried you for nine months

Loved them all that time

Told them that no one could take their place

They are mommy's little boys

The angels to my eyes

The devils to everyone else

The center of my attention

The stars in my sky

They are my little boys!

When they cry- I ask why?

When they play- I let them run wild

When they do good- I reward their work

When they become men

They will still be mommy's little boys.

Dear Ka'Quan

I've loved you from the first time I found out I was pregnant with you. You have always been my first love. I can remember late nights sitting up talking to you in my belly; because you would not let me sleep. Kicking and tumbling and running to the bathroom. I've always made a promise to love you, protect you, and to always rescue you in your time of need.

You're four-teen now and at times I'm scared. You are such a good kid, but these streets scare me, and all I want to do is protect you. Shield you from some unpleasant things in life. We always talk about your football career, and how much you want it, so I will secretly wish you change your career path but openly be your biggest fan.

I believe I've done a good job, kept good role models in your life, and all I wish is for you to be happy. That you always practice safe sex, that we keep our communication table open, that you know my heart, my door and my love will always be open to you. Oh! And that you never use a drug. I have faith in you that you will not let anything or anyone deter you from your dreams of becoming an NFL football player.

LOVE MOM.

Dear Kyril,

In the beginning of finding out I was pregnant my thoughts of you were impure, but as my belly grew and the day I held you in the hospital my heart shifted and you were my special boy. Words could not channel the feeling and emotions I was going through. I loved you then and I love you even more now. I could not imagine my world without you in it.

I remember when you would crawl all over the floor, how your dad and grandma would be upset with me because I would put you in the bed to sleep with me. The hardest time was leaving you when I got sick because I felt like I disappointed you, that I could not be your soldier mom. I want to apologize for not being there during that time, but I promise to always be here now and forever. To guide, watch, love, laugh, smile, cry and call you my sexy guy. I know I tease you about sleeping with me, but those are my best moments; because of the moments I missed.

I know you are going to be or do something great in this lifetime. That you are going to be somebody that people will read about in the history books, and I will sit on the side and simply say, "Job well done son". I love you like no other and only God could separate us.

LOVE MOM.

Katrina Powell

Chapter Three

SURVIVAL

Don't Can't Won't

I don't deal wit numbers

I deal with faces

I do deal with reality

I don't deal with subliminals

I deal with actual conversations

I don't deal with maybes

I do deal with results

I can't tell you your limit

I can only warn you of the consequences

I can't enable you to wonder

can encourage you to grasp the opportunity

I can't walk, talk or feel for you

I can only stand, listen, and pray for you

I won't be a victim

I'll be a survivorI

I will change my outlook towards you and them

I can only hope you change the outlook that you see
towards me

I don't I can't and I won't

Be the bird

That you shoot down.

Katrina Powell

Pain

What is pain?

A feeling

A spot in the middle of your heart

An ache on the body

That medicine cannot cure

A black cloud that always seems to come

At the wrong time

Where does pain hide itself?

In the whisper of our tears

In the words we want to speak

In the guilt of trying and succeeding

Why is there pain?

For us to grieve

For us to know how to hurt

To know that pain comes on a cloud

Leaves on a rainbow.

Skin

The pigment in our epidermis

Made us villains

For centuries

In a world we were forced to be

Hostile to our melanated women

We still don't understand the hatred

Why dismiss us to be with us

Why ridicule what you desire

Does your pale skin not give you enough courage?

Does your forefathers past behavior make you proud

We cannot sob anymore over terrors

We cannot mingle in the doorway with our fears

We as brown shaded queens

Must convey that attacking our body

Does not stop us from articulating

The abuse and not wearing the shame

Turning the knob to justice

Stripping away the silence

That has restrained us from our dominant position

Katrina Powell

We must speak for the slaved generation

We must acknowledge their hardship

We generation Y must announce

That mutilation, rape, and murder

Will not be a part of our future.

Intuition

I am a neighbor

Full of concerns

Questions for any who will answer

My intuition tells me, that you care

I could be wrong-

My nausea tells me I'm on point

That guy you call your friend

Is dead-

Tears are flowing

Pain has covered your heart

Revenge is running through your veins

Now, I'm trying to grasp why?

You put blinders on his choices

You didn't instill the consequences

And you rather spread the grief

Why?

You don't own Ocean or Jackson

It is a block, your name is not tattooed on the street sign

Though you are willing to shed innocent blood

You are not God

Who presents you with the right

To end a life

Who made you the judge and jury

A man with no conscience

Is a man without a soul.

Lost Generation

I come from generation

Of know it alls

Where you can't find a daddy in the house

Where mommy is off chasing pants

Where the grandparents are the foundation of the family

I come from a generation of young death

Where the corners are the enemies

Where your home isn't even a safe haven

Where you watch and you do not speak

I come from a generation

Where fear out way respect

Where an elder would feel safe, now is frighten

Where a child would play in the street, now a parent mourns

Where a community was a family, now is divided

Katrina Powell

I come from a generation
Where the history is lost

I come from a generation
Where materials are pride
It is worth more than a life

I come from a generation
With lots of tears
Where the inside is a lot softer than the outside
When you think they aren't lovable,
They surprise you-
I come from a generation soon to be lost.

Dealer Cycle

A dealer knows his life
What his life will consist of
How they must live their lives
How they must watch and frown all the time
A dealer knows how the dice roll
When they crap to move on
When they dough to be patient
When they tripe to talk a little shit
When they c-low they leaving with the money
A dealer's corner represents his home
A dealer's corner exchange blood money and death
A dealer's corner is his wife
They will protect it and want you to respect it
The dealer's cycle is a lifestyle
It starts from the home atmosphere
It moves into the community environment
It ends with penitentiary or death
Because the few that make it out the cycle
Tell the next generation of dealers
It's grand while you making the money
The house always wins, and you're just the dealer.

Katrina Powell

What It Seems To Me

I seem to be walking in between the trees

Chasing down all the tears and prayers

Fighting all my conflicts and battles

I seem to have dreamy eyes when night falls

Focusing on surviving and tomorrow's journey

Studying the myth and facts of my creed

I blinded myself to walk in the dark

I did not want to see this world

Yes, now that my eyes are open

I wish that I was blind again,

I seem to have abandoned those closest to me

Than those who I can't see nor find;

I seem to communicate with those in my situation better

Than those who are in better circumstances than I-

Questions seem to always enter my mind

Whether I'm dealing with laughter or pain

I'm bent back to where I came from

Reminiscing on the fiddles and the diddles of life

Constantly the same tune runs across the brain waves

I was voiceless

It say,"Pick up your mouth

Pat those feet on concrete ground

Look for your direction

Walk or run until your body won't let you anymore.

Katrina Powell

Dear Officer,

I am a mother, daughter, sister, cousin, lover of a black man

Who will not be silent

About your fear towards our

Caramel, Mocha, Butter, and Blackberry coated men

Your job as an officer is to protect the community you work in

Which means to uphold the laws that you openly took an oath to do

So, I ask why you don't hold your fellow officers accountable

When you see something wrong, Speak on it,

Should not just be a phrase to victims when a criminal act has taken place

Imagine having to discuss with your sons and daughters

How to dress, or what not to wear

Because your clothes can define your innocence or your guilt

That driving with a broken taillight could result in you not returning home

I ask officer,

How can you serve a community you do not know?

Is your job to arrest and fill the jail cells?

Is it to save and build the community you work in?

Officer, When I was little girl

Officers knew the names of parents and the children

Had no problem taking the child home to be
reprimanded:

So officer, I ask you to get to know the lives you police

It will change your fear, it may even remove it

It will show you that we are more alike than different

Especially when it comes to loving our fathers, sons,
brothers, cousins and companions.

We all want to make it home tonight.

Chapter Four

MOTIVATION

Soul Catching

I'm running down the street

The lights are dim

The walk way is empty and quite

I notice I'm alone

Suddenly an unfamiliar voice appears

I ask who?

I ask where?

I turn around slowly

There stands me.

I begin to run again, even faster

The voice yells out to me, I am you

This time I keep on going

Realizing that my legs are gone

I scream for help

I scream to move

I scream to set me free

I'm running down the sidewalk

Reaching for a hand to save me

To protect me from the evil behind me

Chasing me down trying to entrap my soul

Trying to convince me that I'm unworthy

For what God has written in stone for me

Then, I realize

To save my soul is to sacrifice my soul

So, I openly repent my sins

And I begin to walk.

What I Can Not Do

I cannot delay my life

Cause you committed a crime

I cannot skip paying the pse&g bill

Cause you need to converse

I cannot keep dragging my children to visit

Cause your selfishness has put you in a situation

Where you cannot provide or be a parent

I cannot keep accepting collect calls

When I can barely pay the bill

I cannot dream for the both of us

You keep calling these hard times for us

When it isn't hard for you

You got three meals, a bed and lights

They are all FREE and provided by the government

They call you a laborer

I call you a pompous ass

Working for nothing looking for everything

I cannot keep enabling you to ruin my life

I cannot keep promising my children change

If I keep providing for you

I cannot cry anymore

Nor wish for you to change

I can't serve you an ultimatum

The decision has to be your own

I just know I cannot be here

ANYMORE.

Everyday Isn't Good

I awoke this morning

My inner passion tries to fight the anger

Tries to be silent, almost invisible

It bangs loud

My inner self shouts out

Today isn't a good day

The children are screaming

I shove my husband away

I unplug the phone

Turn down the lights

Pray tomorrow is a better day

I cry tears because it balances me

I pray to God because I know he is my friend

I write these words

To let others know

That someone else also knows

Everyday isn't a good day.

I Will Not Lose

I am the battle

It started within me

Worked its way out of me

Made me the crown jewel you see now-

I have battled for love

From mommy, daddy and men

I have battled with insecurities of self

From my lips, and weight, to "is any of me good enough"

I have battled the hatred of

Associates, family and enemies

I have battled knowing too much

To realizing I'm still learning

I have battled betrayal

On the other hand I was rewarded with loyalty

I have battled with my faith

Prayer is a beast it conquers the soul

I have battled with the devil

God is stronger than man

I have battled with cancer.

Dying was not an option.

What, Where, Who, When, Why

What you see at night

Is not always what you see in the light

How you view your indiscretions

Another may label as your original self-worth

Where first expressions aren't erasable

The choices you ultimately make come from within

Who people tell you you're going to be

You always should know that you control the compass of your life

When discouraged and angry

This is where you find hope and prayer

Why everyone around is caught up

You are evolving into that butterfly

What you see at night

Is just what you see in the light.

If I Could

If I could change the sequence of my life

I would

If I could return the kind and the wicked

I would

If I could reconcile the gaps in my family line

I would

If there was ways instead of cruel words

To say you fucked up,

I would use them

If there was a choice between me and your heart

I would choose mine

If there was a chance to beat the haters and,

Smile with grace

I would take it-

With all the if's in this world

Your will must be strong enough

To encourage you on this journey.

Learning to Live

You must learn to live life first
Learn to live with the changes of the days
Learn to lie with a different means of tomorrow
Learn to live with all the choices in your view
May your choices be your heart you follow

Learn to live the road you travel
It may not always be straight and narrow

Learn to live with a heart of forgiveness
A touch can easy a hurting soul
A kiss can mend a broken soul
A hug can encourage another to pass on the JOY

Always learn to live life to its fullest potential
With life ignorance and respect
With life truth and lies
With life told secrets and untold secrets
Always learn to live life with a smile
Life is all what living is supposed to be...

Katrina Powell

Vulnerable

I see a woman who has misplaced

Her trust for convenience

Her loyalty for possessions

Her morals for a momentary smile

I see a woman with no voice

Stripped of her victories

Cause she won't articulate

Her wants and needs

I see a woman whose structure is broken

Due to parasites she has made

Her own embellished self-talk

Her own false display of beauty

I see a woman who is afraid

To transfer into a butterfly

I see a woman that can be a treasure

When she validates herself.

Chapter Five

SELF

Katrina Powell

Seventeen Year Stretch

Opened my eyes on June 3, 1980

Mama carried me across bridges

Saw family and friends come and leave me

Saw sun rises and snowstorms

Saw that I wanted to be a child forever

Yes, questions arose in my mind

Yes, answers arose clearly sometimes

I remember

That dreams kept my brain flowing for seventeen years

I cherish

That my heart still keeps a beat for these seventeen years

I pretend

That's why some of my tears never flowed

I saw pitch black nights,

I saw blanket pallets on hard wooden floors

I saw priceless moments thrown in the garbage

I saw my life fall into the pits

Being the strongest meant tucking and walking on

Seventeen blissful years

I was voiceless

I still cry, pray, wish and struggle

But never grovel or fail to get up;

I felt abused and ignored

But I passed the time with words

I felt abandoned, but alive

I felt destruction, but God worked in my favor

He cleaned windows, so I could see

He fought the shadow of evil away

In all of those seventeen years

I sit here to write this life for you

I opened my eyes on June 3, 1980

God said: This world will be your challenge

Your success will come with a smile.

I Use to

I use to be a young girl searching for intimacy

From a stir down, reading way too much into a hug

Re-quoting "Damn I want take you home and make love"

to "Damn Trina I love you let's go home"

I didn't even live there,

After those three minutes and a shower

I was back lonely and gnawing for my next fix

Looking to share my fears,

My fears just mirrored back at me

Wanting someone to be devoted to me unconditional

When I was self-destructing

From how I viewed myself

To what I thought love was

I was numb

I was blaring my soul

No one came to rescue me

No one paid attention to the girl searching

Because no one could love me

If I could not intimately love myself.

Moms

I'm your daughter
Who is now a mother
Funny, how the story line is the same
When I was expecting more
I didn't realize you were giving what you had
When I was determined to be disobedient
You were more stubborn than I
To keep me focused
When I was spilling evil out my mouth
You were the one smacking down respect
I'm a mother, you are a grandmother
My circumstances in life
Have humbled me, made me grateful
When I could not Hope
You guided me to my Faith
Though my anger within blinded me
I now see God is an equal God
I'm your daughter
You are my mother
We are Moms.

Cancer

I was struck by an arrow carrying cancer

In my prime-

When everything in life was suppose to be about first
experiences

I went from planning my future

TO

Just hoping I would awake tomorrow

I went from play dates with the boys

TO

Hospital rooms and tubes

I could not talk, I just cried

I did not walk, paralyzed by fear

Questions - why me?

I am angry at my father

All I wanted was this to be a lie

That cancer arrow scarred my physical

Sometimes it even pinched my faith

Again, I questioned- why me?

Out of the crowd of millions

I was voiceless

I begin to reflect

God loves me

I have a lesson to learn

I stop questioning God

Started to love God again

In the mix of all this chaos

I've learned the meaning of prayer

As I walk this path in life

I learned many things

The most beautiful lesson is to love

Unconditionally, so when I am blessed

To find love

I will not walk away

I will love that person inside and outside

God will see us through.

Katrina Powell

Transformation

Look at me

I'm a woman

Who has lost her curves

My thickness has vanished

With every needle stick and chemo treatment

I wear battle scars on my neck, legs, and chest

Look at me

I'm a woman

Who cries more now than then

Who laughs every chance I get

Love everyday I'm able to--

Look at me

I'm a woman

Brown skin

Shining in the sunset

Eyes glowing, lips perky

My limp is unique

I was voiceless

People are staring at me

I look and say,

Do you admire what you see?

Or

Are you staring because you are surprised?

I have these beautiful heels on.....

The rain has flooded my eyes

The lighting has exploded my faith

Now the sunburst glows

I smile

Looking at Me

Loving the likeness of me......

Eldest

I'm the oldest sibling

I hold the title of protector

I watch my younger siblings grow

I hope that my wrongs will guide their rights

I, being the oldest, try to lead by example

In my example

I use my uncontrolled life style

Not loving myself enough that it sat inside

Becoming a mother when I wasn't sure

What or how to be

I am big sis

Don't want them confused about love or sex

Becoming a mother way to early

Realizing that grown folks have responsibilities

Way before my mind could adapt to the circumstances

I am big sis

I never preach about following in my footsteps

I preach about walking your own destiny

I push the subject of loving one self

I was voiceless

Growing as a person spiritually, physically, and
emotionally

It's the best story I can share

As the oldest sibling.

Katrina Powell

Bruised In the Inside

I've always known I was special

My heart kept telling me so-

When mommy monster would appear

Rip into my flesh

Each stupid and every smack

Stripping me of my right to glow

I've always known I was special

God kept whispering it to me-

When my daddy did a magic trick

I went searching

To find the magician

Instead I found lonesome, anguish and courage

All within side of me

I've always known I was special

The reflection in the mirror kept reminding me

That for each trauma there would be a star

For each ugly word thrown at me there will be a hug

I was voiceless

For every bruise I wore, they would heal

For the emotions that jumble inside me

God would repair the girl

That has being bruised

That they vanish

With her known

How special she is....

Me

This is me from a girl to a woman

This is me crawling to walking

This is me humbling myself to the human eye

This is me scuffed but still wearable

This is me innocent until proven guilty

This is me brown like cocoa powder

This is me no phony smiles or quick embraces

This is me stern but simple

This is me betrayed and vengeful

This is me hope inside of chaos

This is me parenting alone

This is me facing the monster in the closet

This is me uncontrolled but stable

This is me weeping from relief

This is me sassy with the lips

Beauty that covers my outer wall

A smile that electrifies the heart

That truly loves unconditionally

This is ME.

Chapter Six

DEDICATIONS

Katrina Powell

I am Crying

I am afraid

To lose the loves of my life

I am frustrated

That our young do not value life

I am crying

Cause I lost my sons

Not my birth sons

My village sons

I don't have pictures of my son, just news clippings

I can't recall any memory of them, just the newspaper story

I don't know many of them personally

Although, they are my sons

I am crying because Davonte doesn't get to be a father

I am crying because Darcel doesn't get his wedding day

I am crying because Francisco's friends will never hear his laugh

I am crying because Isaiah's mom will never hug her son

My tears are streaming down the sidewalk

Mixed with innocent blood left on the ground

I was voiceless

I am crying for Ronald, who never made it to senior year

I am crying for Donald who didn't get a chance to meet his new sibling

I am crying for Joshua whose daughter will only know him by memories

I am crying for Darren who will never be able to speak of his accomplishment

I am crying for Larry whose grands will never gain his wisdom

My tears have stained my face, puffed my eyes

Leaving me mourning over the unlawful violence taken over my city

I am crying on behalf of the young black victims

Who names are unknown to me

I am crying on behalf of the young men thinking guns are a solution

I am crying on behalf of Jamal and Shawn who didn't get a chance to choose their fate

I am crying due to the lack of love for black lives

I am crying due to the insufficient support to raise awareness to save black lives

I am crying due to the fact that we are not speaking out about black kings dying

I am crying because I never want to receive that phone call

I am crying because I want my sons to bury me

I am crying for every parent that had to say,

Goodbye to their sons,

Unwillingly.

Ancestors

Our ancestors were stolen away from their homes

Stripped of their native tongue

Shackled and sold

Beaten and killed

All because the color of their skin

They dare not speak back

Whips and overseers

Masters and Misses

Kings and queens now slaves

All because the color of their skin

Our ancestors risked their lives for change

Our ancestors blood is our freedom trail

Our ancestors were people of action

Bestowing upon us prominence in this world

Our ancestors

Buried alive inside the plantation

Taught from the heart

Prayed from their soul

We are our ancestors

We may have never felt a whip across our backs

Cause now the perpetrators use steel handcuffs

We may have never been dehumanized with a water hose

Cause now the perpetrators use the system

We will never know our ancestors agony

For that we should boldly love our skin

Our ancestors

Came by force and stayed to redefine their circumstances

Our skin color made us enemies of America

But it has also made us dominant

You cannot make us vanish

You cannot shame us

Our ancestors

Left a legacy of substance and grace

We must as sons and daughters of kings and queens

Always honor our ancestors.

Man

I have watched a man

Who I have admired

Not because his blood run through my veins

Or

His blue eyes sparkle at me

When he say, "Baby"

I have watched a man

Be the foundation of his family

Through trials and steel

Where a man could have split his corners

Where a man could have trailed off alone,

He fought-

When reduced to tears and pains

He could still be your spirit

I have watched a man,

Drive the highway with speed

Katrina Powell

Tell stories of his younger years

And each time is funnier than the last

I have watched a man

Who has stepped to his own rhythm

Who has scars that are imbedded in his soul

He is a man of loyalty and sacred trust

He is my GRANDPA,

He is divine and

He is MINE!

Every Woman

Every woman has the strength

To crawl, walk and pace themselves

Every woman can strut with their head high

Women pray, it's in our nature to believe

Every woman is a seed

We are the root of the flower

We feed, give shelter and protect

Does it sound like a woman?

Every woman must crawl to stand

To walk on her own

That's why every woman

Should be honored.

Katrina Powell

Sudden

I went without warning

Not giving you time to prepare your goodbyes

I slipped away into my mother's arms

I know you have questions, and want answers

I want you to hold steady to your faith

Know Gods plans for me were greater than my own

You may not understand, why I'm gone and

You may question, why I'm gone

The answer will be, God gave me a date to be born

Date to return to him

When overwhelmed with sadness, seek me

Through your memories

Speak to me, because I don't reply does not

Mean I'm not listening

Know that God will answer all questions

That in time your broken heart will be mended,

The storm will have passed

At the end of the rainbow; I'll be there

Being your guardian angel.

Goodbye

Anyone can say, Hello

It's so easy to bring life into the world

Raise them from infant to adult

Teach them right from wrong

Pray the child represents your hope

Dreams to the stars and flourish in positive thoughts

That's really all a parent can want for

Anyone can say, Hello

After thinking and praying

You'll see they can do well on their own

Don't always need a hand or foot

Good advice is all that you can offer after a while,

Anyone can say, Hello

It's very much harder to say, Goodbye

No one ever considers that word

Or perceives, to say that word to someone special

Not realizing that they would have to,

Ever say, Goodbye

Now I ask everyone,

How to say, Goodbye

Cause everyone can say, Hello!

Katrina Powell

Grandma

Grandma means,

The start of a Generation

A Rare part of the family foundation

She passes our Ancestors stories down

She is a Daughter

She is Mature

She is Amazing

Grandma your love is priceless

Like rare ancient African art

Grandma your smile

Eases away my blues

In our silent conversations

Much was said,

Expressing to me your genuine wisdom

Grandma I'm gonna miss walking into your house

To the smell of lemon and vanilla spice

Grandma who's going to bake for the holidays

Who's going to be speaking knowledge in the room

Who's going hug me and stop time

I was voiceless

Grandma I won't wonder or ask or be selfish

Only because I know how much you love me

Grandma your journey has been filled with,

Great memories and endured trials, now you walk with God

In between the dash it will read,

Grandma's cakes could soak up your aches

Grandma's smile could replace your frown

Grandma's hugs were timeless

Grandma's love is speaking from the pews.

Katrina Powell

Mourn Him

I'm hear

You are no longer,

I can't feel you breathing on my neck

I'm missing the feeling in my nectar

The tears are scrolling down my cheek

In all I keep replaying to myself

Is you aren't here

I'm missing my lover

I'm questioning our time

Why would something so divine

Be taken away from us

My eyes are burning

My heart is filled with despair

When I talk of you- I smile

Unable to contain my composure

The image of you appears

In for that moment

I was voiceless

I realized that you are still spiritual beside me

In my mourning

I forgot that

That our connection hasn't faded

Just your physical has left me

With satisfied memories of us.

Chapter Seven

REFLECTION

A Little Girl Daydream

I grew up,

I would hear

You could be-

The first woman president

Even a doctor

I would say bullshit

In my environment

I would sit on the porch

See the hoodrats

Claim their fame

To be the best "that chick" to touch the streets

I wondered about the dollars

How I could get the local guy

I focused on fake identification

I wrecked my brain

Sketched out my clothes for the club

I pretended to be a stripper

Sliding and lap dancing

This is what my environment produce

This is what I daydream about

How about you?

Katrina Powell

Unattached

How would life be?

If you had everything and did not worry or cry

What kind of life would you lead?

If when you awaken everything laid at your feet

What if you never struggled?

Could not comprehend the feeling of pain

What if lies never existed?

Honor was amongst us all

How could you explain the treasures in the little things?

When all you knew were glamorous things

Where is the mystery in the day?

When you already know what awaits you

Where is the balance in your cipher?

How do you cry?

When do you smile?

What makes you sad?

When do you laugh?

Is this the life you adore?

Is it the life you wish you knew more?

Voice

I'm the voice of the women

Who have been scorned

Bruised on the inside

Where the scar is so deep

No doctor can repair its damage

I'm the voice of the mothers

Struggling from day to day

Wiping tears and making smiles

Preparing children for the world

I'm the voice of wives

Who want to be seen

Who want their men to know their value

As she knows his

I'm the voice of women

Battling with a men

Who thinks being a daddy

Is a part time situation

I'm the voice of single women

Whose unattachment is stirred down as dirty

Katrina Powell

I'm the voice crying for help
I've been beaten to the core
That it hurts to try
I'm the voice pretending that home is blissful
I'm the voice that is soaking in your soul
I'm the voice who is speaking-
If it is not your stone, don't turn it over
If what offended you makes you rewind
It has not offend you, it has made you think
I'm the voice you would like to know
The voice that can either free you
Disturb you
The voice of a woman.

Coward

You are a coward

You have spit on our ancestors remains

You have violated the peace fought for us

You have given society the ammunition

To belittle us as a people

To judge one as all

To take our pain and display it as war

You are a coward

Man or woman

You speak of loyalty- but clearly you have none

You who don't speak- Is guilty as the assassinator of life

You who cannot love themselves

Will always bring hatred in the mist of happiness

You are a coward

Full of ego and pride

No one can laugh at you, No one can disrespect you

You are weak, and preying on one's fear of dying

It doesn't make you a hero

You have become the overseer to your race

Katrina Powell

You are a coward

Because alone you are silent

Cause you are the rapist of unity

Cause every time you take another young black life

You give victory to every racist watching the news

You give every prison owner the opportunity to fill an empty cell

You willingly break hearts of those now mourning love ones

You are a coward

It saddens me, that because of your

COWARDNESS

Tears will fall

Parentless children will be raised, and

Sad for you

Because, I don't know how to hate

So, I love the coward and pray for one.

Black Kings

I address you as kings

Cause you are royalty

I need you to step into the essence of your ancestors

Uncuff yourself from the pain that tugs inside you

The blood that compresses your heart

Is a descendant from greatness

The world wants to keep you hidden

Wants to tarnish the image of the black king

To extinguish the torch inside your spirit,

For they know the gem you are

The world wants to recognize you as, Jeffery Dahmer

When you are Marcus Mosiah Garvey

They choose to see color – You indulge their thoughts

You should see a man and relish that you're a black King

A King they try to cripple with drugs, gangs and guns

Perceive you as a predator – When you are a protector

Name shaming, yelling savage

When you are a survivor

They remove Mr. and replace it with boy

Dishonoring your foundation

You are the teacher of love and war,

The son of a bloodline stained in pain

You are the rise of generational blessings

Black king, as I address you

Your dna contains emperors, pharaohs, and KINGS

Keep walking into your birthright.

World View

When you see me

You think,

Second class citizen

Black woman

Teenage mother

Disable to function

Unattractive to the eye

Because this is what you see

Your view is external

Without any observation

Your conclusion of me

Is below standards

Not to speak or give a kind gesture

I have failed your exam

On the requirements

I am a minority, I rent not own

I take the bus and not drive

Katrina Powell

I collect help from the state, you work

I had children young, why you didn't

I have failed by your standards

You too have failed

Because at the end

We are not judge on materials

But our internal merits

So when you look around

Know someone is judging you to.

Reflection of Self

I pierced into the glass

Trying to get a glimpse

Not recognizing the reflection

I saw a beautiful caramel coated girl

With dark brown hair

Shimmering black eyes

I tried to infiltrate her soul

It was just way to much anger within

Hope happiness finds her, again

I tried to invade the mirror optimistic she would
acknowledged me

Wishing to live long enough to be found

Unlike some of my ancestors

Who had no time to finish what they begun

I turned her soul inside out

I discovered that she smiled all the time

The pain that was buried deep within

That a good cry would purify the wounds

I just needed her to reflect

Times may be difficult

Roads may turn into mazes

Smiles may disappear with the days

Although life will go on as planned

Either here

Or, in the pearly gates of Heaven

We'll all have self reflection.

Life Supposes

Life isn't sweet at all

Life doesn't even make me smile

Life is like a ball of pain

Life is like flames of fire

Torching away hopes, fantasies and dreams

Life supposed to be beautiful

Like spring bud roses

Life supposed to sparkle like uncut diamonds

Instead life is dull, dim and unclear

Of its direction

Life was suppose to be something wonderful

Instead life dealt out a raw pack of wonders.

Chapter Eight

FREE STYLE

Permanent

In the urban jungle

Death is odorless

It rises on the tip of a.m. glory

It lingers in the seams of the minutes

Bodies already embalmed

Live zombies stroll the street corners

In the urban jungle

No one blinks to gun fire

Ears are immune to the sound

Death is not feared

Although its pain still felt

These young folks

Just memorialize it with another t-shirt

In the urban jungle

Death is so frequent

That mourning turns to anger

Anger turns into revenge

That ultimately leads to a vicious cycle

In the urban jungle
Death unmask love
Preparations to say goodbye
Not to you
For you
A coming to heaven walk
Tears and tales

In the urban jungle
Death is the destination
To you, to him or her
That doesn't understand
That these streets
Is the reaper.

Our Magic

I want to tell you a story about magic

The day our sorcery started to dwindle

The moment master called Linda a house nigger

Rose a field nigger

Separating them by shades

Displaying them like unwanted toys

Friends they are

Sisters cannot even sympathize with the others hell

'Cause master has tricked them

As he grin and compliments Linda

When the sunrise, Rose is scorned while onlookers stare

As the sunsets and the moon lights the sky

Linda weeps as master despoils her spirit

As Rose sleeps on bare wood, given to boy

A jealousy grew amongst queens

They stop noticing each other pain

Without notice they adapted to masters evil content for each other

Thinking a pass over loved the life

Of being three shades from white

Still being called a nigger

Dark black became a plague

Our queens was forgetting there magic

The rainbow of their beauty

From albino to ebony

To empathize

To see a woman

To speak life into each other, holding back there tears

To leave judgment

Replace it with compassion

As they stand one brown woman to another

Master tried to dismantle their brown woman magic

Linda said, to Rose I love you

My light skin don't make me love you any less

It's the others

Who hates our brown woman magic!

Switched

Have you ever sketched out your journey?

Framed it by age

Designed it by achievements

Directed it by success gained

I Did.....

Did you ever write your life plans out?

Store your dreams in your heart

Envision life with less uncertainty

Only spoke your desires to God

I Did.....

One act literally changed my grand plans

My objective lens had shifted

The border has doubled

My intentions didn't waver

The realization of my choice grows inside

me

I'm at the point where my promises transitioned

I use to pray for myself

Now, I pray for us

Ten curly toes ten small fingers

Satin brown eyes staring into mine

The scent of cocoa oil

His warm skin clothed into mine

Goal list became a baby registry

College life postponed for daycare

Sightseeing the world rain checked for doctor visits

Late night festivities replace with bed time stories

Soul exploring and midnight chats with my best friend

I learned difficult tasks

Ingrain a love

I never could have imagined

Male Species

Dear male species,

We have adjusted our picture

Of what we thought an amazing male would be to us

We never envision perfect, nor considered you to be experienced

In liken, loving and commitment

Although we did expect you to at least acquire

The things that in twine our lives

We have justified your lies

Explained to ourselves that love undergoes challenges

That your unwillingness to honor us

As the female made from your rib

To undervalue the contentment

We bring into your lives

Dear male specie,

We apologize for the absent parents

We apologize for the woman who broke your heart

Katrina Powell

We apologize for the missed hugs and I love you's

We apologize because no one taught you,

You were worth loving!

We apologize for all the wrongs done to you

Now male specie all that you have endured

We ask, why scorn the woman?

That willfully gives the organ

She can't live without to You.

Assaulted

She was assaulted

Not because she committed a crime

Cause she didn't choose society norm

She paved her own way

Loving another race

For that she was beaten to the concrete

Her innocent blood covered the curb

Face unrecognizable

Blue black bruises dressed her body

Assaulted for loving another human

He was assaulted

Not because he committed a crime

But for simply walking while in love

They threw stones at him,

Homo's not welcome here

Although, the sign on the door read–

Love is the balance of hate

Assaulted for loving what was inside

That he brought outside

She was assaulted

Not because she committed a crime

But for being created

Who knew being biracial

Made her hateable, abortable, unlovable

Prosecuted for love blooming

Assaulted for being priceless

He was assaulted

Not because he committed a crime

But for what appeared in the silhouette

Didn't match what he adored inside

For that he was deemed unwelcomed

Life not sacred

For wanting to change the outside

To pair with his inside

Assaulted for being brave enough to love himself.

Quiet Storm

I know for a fact that being a woman is difficult
I know because I'm a woman

I know that it may feel safe in his arms
Even though I can tell from your eyes that it's dangerous

I know that fleeing out on your own
Is frightening because it's a challenges you to leave your
amenities

I know that having a man
Beats those companionless days

I also know being assaulted and verbally attacked
Is not the behavior you want your
Son to imitate or your daughter to settle for

I know you have blind strength
I know you have unshakeable faith
I just need you to know what I know
So, we can delete the violence against you....

Face Full of Tears

A fall night when the wind was blowing

Love through the dying leaves

It was engaging suitors to unite

Daring people to follow their intuition

Skipping over the fear of being rejected

Removing all self doubt

That night Mother Nature kissed the wind with her
blessings

Within the middle of a steamy summer night

A man with exquisite brown eyes

A rich shade of walnut skin

A trim frame with tone arms

Tasting like sweet fresh picked papaya

Love making dripping from his warm touch

Increasing my heart rate

Daring me to love him

Challenging me to discard my past agony

I was voiceless

As I'm lying in his delicate arms

Engulfed in impressionable emotions

Still staggering with questions

Of love, trust and commitment

Will his forever, be forever?

Unanswered and vulnerable

With a face full of tears

While drenched in our love

I was drowning in my tears

The ones that seeped inside my soul

The ones that never rolled down my face

With every goodbye kiss

With each stab her name drew

With every time he pronounced his love

While walking out the door

Back to where he claim held no purpose

While I held back a face full of tears.

Focus

Focus on the bridges that you cross
Focus on the folks you meet in this life
Focus on those you call an enemy
Make those your friends

Focus on phrases
That you may later repeat in your time
Focus on the light
Never sit to long in the dark
Focus on the gift that God will grant you
Focus on the future for it holds more for you

Focus on what life means to you
Focus on what makes your promises
Come true for you
Focus is the idea
Maintaining it is the key.